THE LITTLE GRAMMAR BOOK

First Aid for Writers

JOE HAYDEN

Marion Street Press

Portland, Oregon

Published by Marion Street Press
4207 S.E. Woodstock Blvd. # 168
Portland, OR 97206-6267
USA
http://www.marionstreetpress.com/

Orders and review copies: 800-888-4741

Author photo © Curt Hart, 2009.

Printed in the United States of America
ISBN 978-1-933338-99-6

Library of Congress Cataloging-in-Publication Data Pending

To all my students

CONTENTS

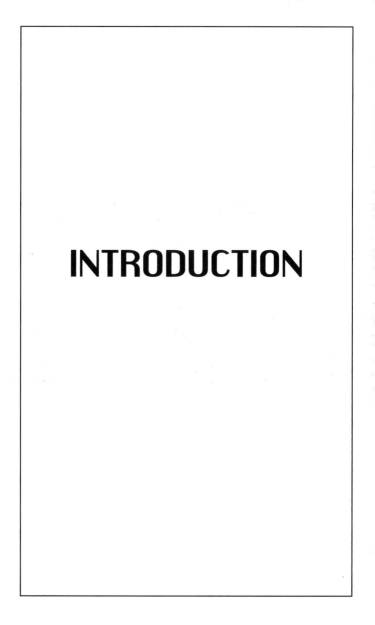

INTRODUCTION

Okay, first, here's the truth that your high school English teacher never told you: language changes, some grammatical rules aren't exactly set in stone, and occasionally the experts disagree.

So does grammar matter? Is it important? Should you bother when so many people use abbreviations and emoticons to send emails or instant-messages to their friends?

Grammar matters because there will always be a need for clear, substantive writing.

Lawyers, bankers, scientists, administrators, journalists and virtually all other professional people and organizations have to communicate with precision and power. Think you'll ever read *imo* or *lol* in a company's stock report? Get real.

There's still a lot of consensus about many of the principles involved in putting words and sentences together. Knowing them will help make you a better writer. Not knowing them will sabotage your best efforts and hurt your reputation.

Most professional writers believe two things about mastering grammar:

1. By itself it won't make you a good writer.

2. But you cannot be a good writer without it.

Let me repeat the second point in case you missed it:

You can't be a good writer without understanding grammar.

Why is that? Grammar is the foundation of writing, the infrastructure that transmits ideas. In fact, think of it like a bridge. However unexciting the engineering that goes into its construction, it won't function—wouldn't be safe—if it were built without regard for materials, support, and stress. Sloppiness is rarely beautiful and often distracting. Nobody's going to notice pretty flags or colorful décor on top when the pillars are crumbling below.

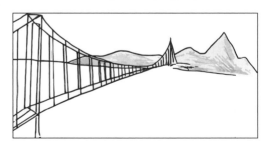

INTRODUCTION

Use faulty grammar and your meaning will fall through and not get where it's going—to its destination, to the people with whom you're trying to communicate.

Grammatical writing is even more crucial in mass communication, in mass media like newspapers, magazines, radio, television and the Internet, because thousands or even millions of readers, listeners or viewers can be misinformed if you put that comma in the wrong place or capitalize the wrong word. Here, all mistakes are magnified, so they don't just haunt you but come back and bite you on the butt.

Worse than simply not communicating, then, with bad grammar you risk being misinterpreted, misunderstood. If your writing stinks, you'll look bad. That perception is totally fair. Most people don't make writing mistakes because grammar is complicated. They make them because they're ignorant and don't care.

"Bad grammar's like a soiled diaper."—Jr.

All writing signals to the audience how reliable—how professional—you are. This applies to whether you work in the media or whether you work as a bank vice president. People judge you by how you communicate, and they'll rightly deem you sloppy and careless if your grammar is sloppy and careless. Your reputation is all you have in this world, so why look like a doofus?

But guess what. Writing is not rocket science. To be honest, it's not much of a science at all. It's really more of an art. And while we can't all be Shakespeares, we can still be pretty good at it.

What's more, we have to be if we want fulfilling jobs that challenge us and pay us well.

These days there's a shortage of employees with strong writing skills. In fact, the need is so dire that companies spend big bucks on remedial training. So this is the upside. Walk into a job as a good writer, and you'll distinguish yourself right away. You'll advance more quickly and get paid more.

Yes, you're hearing it here: talented writers are valuable, and good grammar is actually marketable!

Where do you begin? Writing effectively starts with learning grammar, and fortunately grammar is something anyone can eventually master. Indeed, while the process may not happen overnight, it is rather simple. It just involves memorizing a small bunch of rules, then applying them over and over again.

Here in this book, then, are the guidelines for correcting and avoiding some of the most common grammatical problems. Obviously, this is not a comprehensive reference book. It's just a boost to get you back on the right track with some simple reminders. And by concentrating on a few crucial issues, it helps you separate the monumental from the trivial. It won't waste your time. It might even show you that learning grammar is not that tough.

Then when you're ready to raise your game to the next level, as any aspiring professional aims to do, check out the recommended books listed on p. 88. These books won't just make you a better writer; they'll make you downright dangerous.

That's because strengthening your writing helps you say what you mean, and that, in turn, lets you stand out from the crowd—no small thing in this noisy, confusing world. Good writing, you see, enables audiences to notice you and to understand you.

And that's really the best reason to improve your grammar:

Communicating

clearly

helps

YOU

matter.

HOW TO USE THIS BOOK

What this book is

This book is a bare-bones summary of the most basic grammatical problems and how to fix them. It's divided by chapters to address each issue and does so in just a few pages. The point is to give writers the quickest, most efficient help available—all by just flipping a few pages.

What this book isn't

It isn't comprehensive, and because it's a simplified version it may gloss over some of the thornier and more complicated issues. That's okay. What I hope this book does is to inspire you to improve. Eventually, you should get other reference books, including a more thorough book on grammar. Mine is designed merely to break the ice and get you moving.

Tips

This book can be used either to render first aid in the field or as a book to browse at your leisure. If you have time for the latter, or if you're really struggling with one issue or the other, you should really study the sections on the **parts of speech** and on **clauses**. All grammatical rules are built on this foundation, and if you don't understand the difference between a verb and an adverb, you can hardly expect to learn what makes something a complete sentence and something else a sentence fragment.

The exercises at the end of the grammar chapters are meant to give you practice. Learning anything well involves actively doing something. This practice helps set the principle you've just acquired and "cements" it through the process of repetition. You need reps. The more of them you get the better you'll become.

BODY PARTS

THE 8 PARTS OF SPEECH

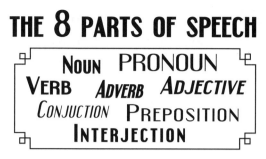

What "Parts"?

The building blocks of any language are the parts of speech—different sorts of words categorized by their function, by what they do in a sentence. You can't understand grammar without knowing these.

Cast of characters

There are eight major parts of speech in English. Here they are and what they do:

1. **Noun—a person, place, or thing**

   EXAMPLES: *Richard, philosophy, TV, cake, Miami, marriage*

2. **Pronoun—stands in place of a noun**

   EXAMPLES: *I, you, he, she, it, we, you, they, one, who, which, that*

3. **Verb—embodies the action**

   EXAMPLES: *go, does, is trying, fights, think, guess, kissed, saw, ask, talked, become, sit, die, hope*

4. **Adverb—modifies (describes) a verb, an adjective, or another adverb**

   EXAMPLES: *well, quickly, really, very, seldom, then, however, smoothly*

5. **Adjective—modifies (describes) a noun**

    EXAMPLES: *blue, quiet, friendly, five, hungry, strong, cheerful, serrated, high-definition, a* or *the* (which are also known as "articles")

6. **Conjunction—joins words, phrases, clauses**

    COORDINATING CONJUNCTION: *and, but, or, for, so, yet*
    SUBORDINATING CONJUNCTION: *after, although, because, before, if, since, though, unless, when, whether, while*

7. **Preposition—shows the connection (in time or space) between two or more things**

    EXAMPLES: *around, at, between, by, for, in, near, on, over, through, to, under, with*

8. **Interjection—expresses unessential information but attracts attention**

    EXAMPLES: *gosh, hey, no, um, well, yes*

Double duty

Some words can be more than one part of speech.

> *This and that* can be pronouns: *This is crazy. That is too.* They can also be adjectives: *This system is crazy. That system isn't.*

> *Fast* can be an adjective: *That's a fast car.* It can also be an adverb. *He drove fast.*

> *Here* and *there* can be adverbs. *He went here; she went there.* They can also be pronouns. *Here is what I'm saying: there is no way I'll do it.*

> Numbers can be nouns: *Two were here.* They can also be adjectives: *Two friends are coming over.*

CLAUSES AND SENTENCES

Clauses

A clause is a group of words with both a *subject* and a **verb**.

Clause types

Main (or independent) clauses—These *can* stand alone as a complete sentence.

> EXAMPLES: *She* <u>sings</u>. *I* <u>am going</u> to the store at 6 o'clock. *Life*<u>'s</u> hard. *You*'<u>re</u> right. *Are* <u>you</u>?

Subordinate (or dependent) clauses—These *can't* stand alone; they must be attached to the beginning or the end of a main clause.

> EXAMPLES: ***Because*** she sings.... ***Although*** I am going to the store at 6:00.... ***If*** life's hard.... ***While*** you're right...

Subordinate conjunctions (*because, although, if, while*) make these clauses subordinate—dependent. If you remove the conjunctions, they would be main clauses. If you keep them, they need to be connected to a main clause, or else you'll have a sentence fragment. *Because she sings* is not a complete sentence.

One exception to main clauses

One exception to the definition of a main clause is a command or imperative. Even though it looks as though it's missing a subject, the *you* is implied.

> *Please go.*
>
> *Leave me alone.*
>
> *Shut up.*
>
> *Let's do it.*
>
> *Stop.*

These examples are all grammatically complete sentences.

Words that make the clause subordinate

1. Subordinating conjunctions: *although, because, since, while*
[See p. 20 for more examples.]

SUBORDINATE CLAUSE: *while the soldier slept...*

2. Relative pronouns: *that, which, who, whoever*

SUBORDINATE CLAUSE: *whoever gets here first...*

SUBORDINATE CLAUSE: *...that he would help.*

SUBORDINATE CLAUSE: *...that she's the best.*

To make subordinate clauses into complete sentences, just add a **main clause** to the beginning or end:

COMPLETE SENTENCE:

> *There can be no doubt*   *that she's the best*.
> MAIN CLAUSE   SUBORDINATE CLAUSE

COMPLETE SENTENCE:

> *That she's the best*   *there can be no doubt*.
> SUBORDINATE CLAUSE   MAIN CLAUSE

THE DIRTY DOZEN

SENTENCE FRAGMENTS

What is a sentence fragment? *It is part of a sentence that can't stand alone.*

Types: *Which parts can't stand alone?*

1. Nouns or noun phrases (*"a very talented basketball player, his coach, and his teammates"*)

2. Verbs or verb phrases ("*running after the bus and double-checking the time on her watch*")

3. Subordinate clauses (*"although I'm tired"* or *"because they haven't slept in 24 hours"*)

These clauses are subordinate (or dependent) because of a subordinating conjunction—a connecting word like "although" or "because."

Review: *What makes a sentence complete, independent? You generally need a subject and verb. And make sure you don't put a subordinating conjunction (such as "while," "if," "although," or "since") before them.*

Examples of fragments:

EXAMPLE: *Goes to the store* (verb phrase)

EXAMPLE: *Getting off to a bad start* (verb phrase)

EXAMPLE: *Two sweaters, a jacket, and a pair of jeans* (noun phrase)

EXAMPLE: *Because she's hungry* (subordinate clause)

EXAMPLE: *Since he graduated from high school* (subordinate clause)

How to fix

Turning a fragment into a complete sentence is easy. All you need is a main clause: a subject and then a verb to go with it. That's it.

SUBJECT + VERB = COMPLETE SENTENCE

Examples fixed:

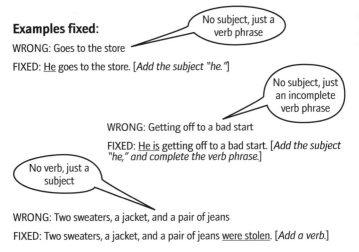

WRONG: Goes to the store

No subject, just a verb phrase

FIXED: <u>He</u> goes to the store. [*Add the subject "he."*]

No subject, just an incomplete verb phrase

WRONG: Getting off to a bad start

FIXED: <u>He is</u> getting off to a bad start. [*Add the subject "he," and complete the verb phrase.*]

No verb, just a subject

WRONG: Two sweaters, a jacket, and a pair of jeans

FIXED: Two sweaters, a jacket, and a pair of jeans <u>were stolen</u>. [*Add a verb.*]

1. SENTENCE FRAGMENTS

WRONG: Because she's hungry

No main clause, just a subordinate one

FIXED: <u>She ordered the cheeseburger</u> because she's hungry. [*Add a main clause.*]

No main clause, just a subordinate one

WRONG: Since he graduated from high school

FIXED: Since he graduated from high school, <u>he's been looking for a job</u>. [*Add a main clause.*]

Crucial reminder

A complete sentence must have a **MAIN CLAUSE**. If all you have is a subordinate clause, that's not correct. You'll recognize a subordinate clause from its subordinate conjunction. Here are the most common of them: *after, although, as, because, before, if, since, though, unless, when, while*. If one of these precedes a clause (a subject-verb combo), it's probably a subordinate clause, meaning it can't stand on its own and you have a fragment.

COMPLETE SENTENCE: *I went.*

SENTENCE FRAGMENT: *After I went.*

COMPLETE SENTENCE: *She stayed.*

SENTENCE FRAGMENT: *Because she stayed.*

One exception to main clauses

One exception to the definition of a main clause is a command or imperative. For example, *please go* or *leave me alone* is a complete sentence, even though each looks as though it's missing a subject.

Unlike subordinating conjunctions, coordinating conjunctions (*and, but, or, for, so, yet*) don't affect a main clause. She stayed is just like "and she stayed." Both are main clauses. Adverbs (*however, therefore, then*) function the same way. "I went" and "however, I went" are both main clauses, too. So adverbs and coordinating conjunctions generally keep main clauses complete.

Test Yourself

Which of the following examples are sentence fragments, and which are complete sentences?

1. Tell her once more.

2. Finding it out only yesterday.

3. Goes it alone.

4. Although I'm not really sure.

5. You are?

6. I am.

7. Give me a break.

8. If I were you.

9. Leaving first thing in the morning and buying a cup of coffee at work.

10. Just try it.

2 FUSED SENTENCES

What's a fused sentence? *It's two or more sentences smashed together without proper punctuation.*

Aliases: *It's also called a run-on sentence, maybe because one sentence is running over another. Either way, you have a wreck on your hands.*

EXAMPLES

1. *I'm not going to the game she will.*

2. *He brought wings to the party she brought pizza.*

How to fix

1. Put a period between them. •

or

2. Put a semicolon between them. **;**

or

2. FUSED SENTENCES

3. Put a comma and a coordinating conjunction between them.

, AND

, BUT

, OR

, FOR

, SO

, YET

4. Put a subordinating conjunction between them.

WHILE

ALTHOUGH

BECAUSE

SINCE

IF

Examples fixed

Wrong: I'm not going to the game she will.

> __Right__: I'm not going to the game. She will.

> __Right__: I'm not going to the game; she will.

> __Right__: I'm not going to the game, but she will.

> __Right__: I'm not going to the game because she will.

Wrong: He brought wings to the party she brought pizza.

> __Right__: He brought wings to the party. She brought pizza.

> __Right__: He brought wings to the party; she brought pizza.

> __Right__: He brought wings to the party, and she brought pizza.

> __Right__: He brought wings to the party while she brought pizza.

Students often wind up with fused sentences when they include an adverb like "now," "then," "however," or "therefore," because they forget to which main clause it belongs. Those are perfectly good words, but they can't join sentences.

2. FUSED SENTENCES

Reminders

Most sentences combine a subject and a verb. So when you're working with more than one of these combinations, be careful. If you want to keep them together in the *same* sentence, you have three options: use a subordinating conjunction, use a comma and a coordinating conjunction, or else use a semicolon.

Related References

Also see *conjunctions* in "The 8 Parts of Speech" (p. 9).

Also see *main clauses* and *subordinate clauses* in "Clauses and Sentences" (pp. 11–12).

Test Yourself

Correct the following fused sentences:

1. The police arrested a suspect last night they haven't yet released his name.

2. Here is the money I owe you can use it for whatever you want.

3. "I feel good I knew that I would."—James Brown

4. He asked her out I heard she said, "No, but dream on."

5. My roommate bought all this beer therefore it's now my favorite.

6. Give me a break I don't know.

7. Houston's point guard scored 28 points the power forward turned in a dozen more.

8. The Marine sniper set the scope on his M40 then he squeezed the trigger.

9. I emailed you last week now you're getting back to me.

10. She's going to law school her sister is a licensed electrician.

③ COMMA SPLICES

A comma's like a weak nail.

What is it?

A comma splice happens when you join two clauses badly. What's the mistake? It's thinking that a comma alone can bind or splice two main clauses. A comma can't do that by itself. Think of it as a weak nail. To join main clauses you need something a lot stronger.

EXAMPLES

I'm going, you're staying.

He took the last donut, she drank all the milk.

Snow fell for six hours, it eventually stopped but became icy at night.

Each of these clauses is a main clause, a complete sentence. *I'm going* is a perfectly grammatical sentence. But you can't attach it to another main clause unless you have the right "joiners," the right adhesive or fastener.

Conjunction

The rules

To combine two main clauses in the same sentence, you have three options: (a) use a semicolon; (b) use a subordinating conjunction; (c) use a coordinating conjunction and a comma.

People usually create a comma splice with the last of these. But remember: a comma alone won't join two main clauses grammatically. You need a coordinating conjunction, too.

How to fix

1. Replace the comma with a period. •

or

2. Replace the comma with a semicolon. ;

or

3. COMMA SPLICES

3. Put a comma and a coordinating conjunction between the clauses.

, AND

, BUT

, OR

, FOR

, SO

, YET

4. Put a subordinating conjunction between the clauses.

WHILE

ALTHOUGH

BECAUSE

SINCE

IF

Examples fixed

Comma Splice: I'm going, you're staying.

> **Fixed**: I'm going; you're staying.

> **Fixed**: I'm going, but you're staying.

> **Fixed**: I'm going because you're staying.

Comma Splice: He took the last donut, she drank all the milk.

> **Fixed**: He took the last donut; she drank all the milk.

> **Fixed**: He took the last donut, and she drank all the milk.

> **Fixed**: He took the last donut while she drank all the milk.

Comma Splice: Snow fell for six hours, it eventually stopped but became icy at night.

> **Fixed**: Snow fell for six hours; it eventually stopped but became icy at night.

> **Fixed**: Snow fell for six hours, and while it eventually stopped it became icy at night.

3. COMMA SPLICES

The adverb hazard

Watch out for adverbs—words like *then, therefore, however.*
These look like conjunctions, but they're not. One of the most
frequent comma splices occurs when people try to join two main
clauses with "however."

Comma Splice: The mayor decided to resign, however, he won't
announce it until Monday.

> **Fixed**: The mayor decided to resign. However, he won't an-
> nounce it until Monday.

> **Fixed**: The mayor decided to resign; however, he won't an-
> nounce it until Monday.

> **Fixed**: The mayor decided to resign, but he won't announce
> it until Monday.

Commas alone don't
join main clauses. They
also need a coordinat-
ing conjunction (*and,
but, or, for, so, yet*) to
do that. It's obviously
important to know
whether your clauses are main ones or not. Just remember
that main clauses are grammatically correct sentences. They
have a subject and a matching verb.

Test Yourself

Which of the following are comma splices? Fix those that are.

1. Today the team won its first game of the season, it's about time.

2. My car gets 35 miles per gallon, what about yours?

3. Eric put 12 burgers on the grill, the most that he's ever tried to cook.

4. You cell phone isn't working, mine is.

5. The fire fighter got on the truck, however, he forgot his helmet.

6. I'm tired, I know you must be.

7. We drove to New Orleans last night, a city where something's always happening.

8. The movie had just started, then I had to go to the bathroom.

9. She bought two tickets, then got a third one for her roommate.

10. Please go, don't forget your keys.

4

OTHER COMMA PROBLEMS

Direct Address, Interjections, and Unessential Phrases

Commas frequently cause problems in English grammar. This chapter will focus on three common ways this piece of punctuation gets botched and ends up littering the roadway:

1. Direct address

2. Interjections

3. Unessential phrases

1. Direct address

John, listen to me.

When you directly address someone in your writing, you need to signal readers to let them know. A comma is the signal. Think of the comma in this case as a raised hand, one being used to get the other person's attention:

John,   **listen to me.**

Incorrect: John listen to me.

Correct: John, listen to me.

In this example, you're addressing John. We know that by the comma after his name. It would also be correct to write *Listen to me, John.* Either way, his name has to be separated from the rest of the sentence. Otherwise, we'll think it's the subject and that it's supposed to go with the verb. *John listen to me* looks as though the writer's saying that John *is* listening to him, although in that case it would have to be *John listens to me.* See the confusion? That's why we use the comma.

4. OTHER GRAMMAR PROBLEMS

Here are two other examples:

Wrong: Everybody dance now.
   Correct: Everybody, dance now.

Wrong: Go Tigers!
   Correct: Go, Tigers!

Again, you separate the people you're addressing from the rest of the sentence with a comma. Without it, we'll think you're saying that everybody is dancing now, not that you're telling everybody to dance. Or, in the second example, we might believe you're saying that the Tigers *are* going somewhere, rather than that you want them to do so.

2. Interjections

"Hey, you, get off of my cloud."—Rolling Stones

Interjections are unessential words thrown into a sentence for extra flavor, color, or emotion—words like *ah, aw, gosh, hey, no, oh, well, wow, yes*. They need to be separated from the rest of the sentence with commas.

Note that *well* can be an adjective or an adverb, too. (*She played well.*) But when it's used as an interjection, it's cordoned off with punctuation. (*Well, I don't care what he says.*) Without the comma, it would look like an adverb describing the verb *care*, which isn't the case.

3. Unessential phrases

Essential phrases are ones you can't remove without changing the meaning or damaging grammar. But *unessential phrases* are different. They're a lot less important. They're like parenthetical comments, which add extra information but aren't crucial or indispensable. These take commas.

Actually, **parentheses** are a good way to remember them. Imagine the commas as parentheses. No one puts integral information in parentheses. Commas work the same way, and when they're in the middle of the sentence they come in pairs—just like parentheses.

The most common kind of unessential phrase usually involves a complete date or city-state combination.

Month, day, year
On Nov. 4, 2008, Barack Obama was elected president of the United States.

In this example, 2008 might be helpful, but it's not essential. The sentence is still true without giving the year: *On Nov. 4 Barack Obama was elected president of the United States.*

4. OTHER GRAMMAR PROBLEMS

City and state

We left Memphis, Tennessee, and drove to Little Rock, Arkansas.

In this example, the states' names are helpful but not essential. It would be fine to write the following sentence: *We left Memphis and drove to Little Rock*. Again, the commas show parenthetical information. So they function like parentheses and come in pairs.

Another type of unessential phrase is one that **identifies someone or something**.

EX. 1 *The mayor of Memphis, A.C. Wharton, spoke to the press last night.*

In this example, the mayor's actual name isn't absolutely necessary. The sentence still holds without it: *The mayor of Memphis spoke to the press last night.*

EX. 2 *A.C. Wharton, the mayor of Memphis, spoke to the press last night.*

Here we flipped the components, and the same principle holds. Again, the phrase surrounded by commas isn't crucial. We could take it out, and the sentence would still make sense: *A.C. Wharton spoke to the press last night.*

EX. 3 *Mayor A.C. Wharton spoke to the press last night.*

Note that there are no commas around the name. That would imply we could take it out, but we can't; without A.C. Wharton, the sentence would sound mangled: *Mayor spoke to the press last night.* You'd have to revise the sentence.

Relative clauses—those beginning with a relative pronoun like who, which, or that—also frequently involve unessential clauses.

> UNESSENTIAL: *The company, which celebrated its centennial last year, is filing for bankruptcy.*

It would be perfectly fine to remove the middle passage and rewrite the sentence this way: *The company is filing for bankruptcy.* So the commas work like parentheses, giving you additional information you may want to know. But the sentence is coherent and sensible without it.

> ESSENTIAL: *The company that celebrated its centennial last year is filing for bankruptcy.*

Here you are singling out one company from others, and so you need the phrase in the middle to specify which—just the one that celebrated its centennial last year.

So what this area of grammar

comes down to, then, is

YOU—your intention.

WHAT DO YOU MEAN?

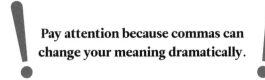

Pay attention because commas can change your meaning dramatically.

ESSENTIAL: *He dislikes lawyers who are ambulance chasers.*

UNESSENTIAL: *He dislikes lawyers, who are ambulance chasers.*

Both of these are correct, but their meanings are very different. In the first example, he dislikes *only* those lawyers who are ambulance chasers. In other words, he likes some lawyers but dislikes others. It's restrictive, carefully limiting whom he likes and whom he doesn't. The second example is unrestrictive or parenthetical, so you could take out the relative clause without affecting the gist: he doesn't like lawyers, any lawyers, because evidently he thinks they're *all* ambulance chasers.

Some complications

As noted before, much of the punctuation depends on what you mean and what the facts are. That's also true in most of these cases, too:

A. His wife, Gloria, likes that movie.

B. His friend John likes it, too.

C. His sister Julie hasn't seen it yet.

A. Definitely unrestrictive

Because he can legally have only one wife, it's not necessary to specify which one. So adding the wife's name is just parenthetical information. It's not essential.

B. Probably unrestrictive

Because people generally have more than one friend, you don't have to specify which one. In fact, if you were to put commas around the name, it might imply that John is his only friend.

C. Depends on the facts

We have to assume from the lack of a comma that he has more than one sister. Had there been commas around the name, it would imply that Julie is his only sister.

Review

So essential phrases have to be woven seamlessly into the fabric of the sentence. You don't put commas around them. Unessential phrases are parenthetical ones. They're dispensable, and the commas show that what's inside is not vital for understanding the sentence.

Test yourself

Which of the following sentences are correctly punctuated, and which aren't? Fix the latter.

1. The company was founded on March 12, 1974 in Milwaukee Wisconsin.

2. Well that's what you think.

3. Dad can you hear me now?

4. Go, team!

5. Her husband Mike joined us at the restaurant.

6. Barack Obama the 44th president of the United States was born in Hawaii.

7. Derrick wants to be a stand-up comic which is not what you'd expect from him.

8. Governor, John Smith, visited our city during the summer.

9. Jay-Z, whose real name is Shawn Carter, grew up in Brooklyn.

10. The movie made $60 million over the weekend which wasn't a surprise to those of us who saw it.

⑤ MISPLACED MODIFIERS

What is it? A misplaced modifier is a word or phrase out of place. The result is that it winds up describing (modifying) the wrong thing, thus changing the meaning.

> _Having just given birth to eight puppies_, my friend Tom gave the tired mother a bowl of water.

Does something sound weird about that sentence? It should. My friend Tom did not just give birth to eight puppies. Whatever follows the underlined phrase has to be the thing that did—a tired mother.

How to fix

You can move the modifying phrase, or you can change what comes afterward.

> CORRECTED: _Having just given birth to eight puppies, the tired mother was given a bowl of water by my friend Tom._

> CORRECTED: _My friend Tom gave the tired mother a bowl of water after she had just given birth to eight puppies._

5. MISPLACED MODIFIERS

The rule
Put modifiers next to the thing they modify.

Other examples

M.M.: *After a look around the building, Reggie's words are proved true.*

FIXED: <u>After a look around the building, you can see that Reggie's right</u>.

FIXED: <u>Reggie's words are proved true by a look around the building</u>.

The first sentence makes it sound as though Reggie's words had a look around the building. If you're going to keep the opening phrase, you need to change what immediately follows.

M.M.: *Looking through the windows of the building, workers can be seen painting walls and installing blue light fixtures.*

FIXED: <u>Looking through the windows of the building, you can see workers painting walls and installing blue light fixtures</u>.

Workers weren't looking through the windows of the building. This writer is describing what he did to see the workers. Again, what follows that long descriptive phrase must be the thing that's being described.

M.M.: *For those missing home, soup and biscuits are offered, as well as fried chicken and mashed potatoes.*

FIXED: <u>For those missing home, soup and biscuits, as well as fried chicken and mashed potatoes, are offered</u>.

Here's a case in which someone forgot to add the fried chicken and mashed potatoes to the sentence, so they were just lumped in at the end. The problem is that they're orphaned like that—stranded from the other foods (the soup and biscuits) being offered. Keep the items together.

Position matters

- <u>*Only*</u> *I see this computer screen.*

- *I <u>only</u> see this computer screen.*

- *I see <u>only</u> this computer screen.*

All three of these sentences appear grammatically correct. But whether they really are or not depends on what the writer means. *Only* limits the meaning in each case, so where it goes is a crucial matter.

Only I see this computer screen limits the <u>subject</u>, so it means I'm the only one who sees it. *I only see this computer screen* limits the <u>verb</u>, so it means I don't perceive it any other way but by sight. *I see only this computer screen* limits the object, so it means there might be other things that are visible, but this is the only one I'm able to see.

Be precise. Put *only* <u>immediately</u> before what it modifies (describes).

Test yourself

Correct the following sentences.

1. Heading upstairs to escape the smell of detergents, a hall with shields hanging at eye-level draws visitors to the north side of the floor.

2. Looking around, almost every table is filled with at least one person.

3. Students rest on benches reading books and sit on sidewalks browsing their laptops.

4. An elderly woman sits in the center of the room eating chicken constantly turning her head from left to right as she watches others.

5. They are all dressed in team uniforms talking among themselves.

6. While standing outside, 15 minutes went by as the man watched in horror.

7. Sitting outside the library, students walked past silently.

8. She donated old clothes and several cans of food to the shelter, along with a new bicycle.

9. We had a great time singing and dancing at the party, not to mention catching up with old friends.

10. Tearing through the city and ripping the roof off a restaurant, my dad videotaped the tornado's destructive path.

❻
SUBJECT-VERB
MISMATCHES

Subjects are from Mars.
Verbs are from Venus.
—————————
But they still have to match.

Matches and mismatches

Subjects and verbs are like two people in love with little in common but who are blissfully happy together. They may look different, but the relationship works.

Or take an electronics analogy. They're like interlocking ends of a cable, because you can't fit two prongs together, nor can you do much with two receptacles. You need one of each to make the connection.

What is it?

A subject-verb mismatch happens when you pair a subject with the wrong verb. In that case, the subject and the verb don't agree.

6. SUBJECT-VERB MISMATCHES

Think of the cable comparison. Only now there are two types of receptacles and two types of prongs:

| *singular subject* | *singular verb* | *plural subject* | *plural verb* |
| **Time...** | **...flies.** | **Teachers...** | **...advise.** |

To build a sentence you have to know how to connect these pairs. It's not hard when you know the rules.

The Rules

1. Singular subjects—one person, one thing—usually require a verb with an *s* at the end.

   EXAMPLE: *The student **goes** into the store.*

2. Plural subjects—two or more persons or things—require a verb <u>without</u> an *s* at the end.

   EXAMPLE: *Two students **go** into the store.*

3. The pronoun *you* always acts like a plural noun, whether it refers to one or many.

   EXAMPLES: *You **are** the love of my life. You **are** all weird.*

Watch out for falling objects!

It's simple, right? Well, things get complicated if you don't know how to recognize the subject of a sentence. That's especially true when there are prepositional phrases lurking around the real subject.

> WRONG: *The cause of the fires haven't been determined.*

> RIGHT: <u>The cause of the fires **hasn't** been determined</u>.

In this example, ***cause*** (*not fires*) is the subject. The word *fires* is the object of a preposition (*of*), and objects can't be subjects. To locate the subject, first find the complete verb and ask yourself who or what's doing it. Who or what *hasn't been determined*? The answer is the **cause** *of the fires*.

Other traps

1. When the subject consists of two singular nouns separated by the conjunction *or*, the verb will be singular, too.

WRONG: *Either the councilman or the mayor **get** the worst publicity in town.*

RIGHT: <u>Either the councilman or the mayor **gets** the worst publicity in town.</u>

Think of it like a math equation. The subject is not one + one.

It's one OR one—that is, one or the other but not both.

1 *OR* 1. . . STILL = 1

If one is plural and one is singular, the one closer to the verb takes priority. *Either the mayor or the council members know.*

2. Don't be fooled by book or movie titles. A title is still one thing (singular).

WRONG: Syd and Nancy ***are** a cool movie.*
RIGHT: <u>*Syd and Nancy* **is** a cool movie.</u>

3. Despite the *s* on the end, many words like physics, politics, or economics are singular and take a singular verb.

WRONG: *Politics **are** my favorite subject.*
RIGHT: <u>Politics **is** my favorite subject.</u>

Except for the preceding examples, most nouns ending in *s* that are not in the possessive case are plurals. Plural nouns require plural verbs, which do not end in *s*. So if you have both a subject and a verb ending in *s*, look out. You might have a mismatch.

Reminders

Locate the subject of the sentence by determining who or what is doing the action (the verb). Make sure if the subject is singular, its verb is too. If it's plural, make the verb plural as well. It's just a simple matter of connection.

Related References

See *nouns* in "The 8 Parts of Speech" (p. 9).

See *verbs* in "The 8 Parts of Speech" (p. 9).

6. SUBJECT-VERB MISMATCHES

Test Yourself

Correct the following sentences:

1. "Joints & Jam" are the name of a song by the Black Eyed Peas.

2. My friends all likes the movie. My girlfriend do too.

3. Economics are the first subject I got a C in at school.

4. The reasons for her reaction is simple: I let her down.

5. Either he or John go, or you and she goes.

6. The days of summer is almost over.

7. Thirty pounds of high-grade marijuana was confiscated in the raid.

8. The best argument for these ideas were missed by bloggers and mainstream journalists alike.

9. You's joking, right?

10. Two players on the team was suspended last night.

7

SUBJECT-PRONOUN MISMATCHES

What kind of mismatch?

Subject-pronoun mismatches often involve confused counting—usually over whether the subject is plural or singular.

The #1 culprit

The most common such mistake is a singular subject but a plural pronoun.

> MISMATCH: *Someone said they enjoyed the debate.*
>
> *Someone* (hint: *one*) is singular. So the pronoun has to be singular as well. *They* isn't singular. You need a word that is.
>
> CORRECTED: <u>One man said he enjoyed the debate</u>.
>
> CORRECTED: <u>Someone praised the debate</u>.

Yes, you could write "he or she," which would be both grammatically and politically correct. But it would be stylistically clumsy. And good writers try hard to avoid torturous phrasing.

7. SUBJECT-PRONOUN MISMATCHES

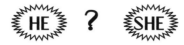

To avoid writing "he or she" or "his or her," either specify the subject in the singular, or change the subject to the plural, which allows you to use "they."

> AWKWARD: *The teacher said that each student must do his or her best.*
>
> FIXED: <u>The teacher said that all students must do their best</u>.

The challenge

As you can tell, the trick is to pay close attention to what the subject is and to make sure your pronoun agrees. The problem is common confusion over several words and what number they take. Let's look at some typical troublemakers.

Deceptively singular words

The following words are singular, meaning they take a singular pronoun (*it, he, she*), possessive adjective (*its, his, her*), or verb (*says, plans, announces*).

Group A: Words that represent several people but are **still singular**

Board	Group
Committee	Organization
Company	School
Council	Senate
Family	University

Group B: Words that may sound vague or inexact but are **still singular**

Anyone	Neither
Each	One
Either	Person
Everybody	Someone
Everyone	Somebody

Examples

MISMATCH: *The company said **they** had a very profitable third quarter.*
FIXED: <u>The company said **it** had a very profitable third quarter</u>.

MISMATCH: *The school announced today that **they** will hold classes as scheduled.*
FIXED: <u>The school announced today that **it** will hold classes as scheduled</u>.

MISMATCH: *Ask anyone, and **they'll** tell you the same thing.*
FIXED: <u>Ask **most people**, and they'll tell you the same thing</u>.

Fixing the third example is the typical remedy for treating Group B terms—words like *anyone, everyone,* or *someone*: it's easier just to replace it with a clearly plural noun.

7. SUBJECT-PRONOUN MISMATCHES

Pointers

If a word has an obvious singular and plural (*company, companies*), make sure you treat each accordingly. It might help to specify the person or persons involved. And if you really like the plural pronoun, you could say *committee members*, for example.

Group B words require exact matches, too, so if you can't find a smooth-sounding singular to go with it, change it to the plural.

Test yourself

Fix the following sentences:

1. Ask the average person, and they'll tell you they love junk food.

2. No one wants to lose their job.

3. The sorority tried to raise money for their favorite charity.

4. A spokesperson for the group said they would try to reschedule.

5. Everyone deserves their fair opportunity.

6. The Senate passed the bill unanimously, the first time they agreed on anything all year.

7. The board shared their views before the vote.

8. Someone's in a bad mood, aren't they?

9. One wonders if they have what it takes to go the distance.

10. Coca Cola has no plans to move their headquarters.

GETTING POSSESSIVE

Problems With the Possessive Case

What is it? *The possessive case shows that someone or something belongs to someone or something else. It shows* ***possession***.

Examples

> 1. *That woman's Ferrari is red.*
>
> 2. *The car's interior is black.*

In the examples above, the words *woman's* and *car's* are in the possessive case.

The Rules

Possessive nouns usually call for 2 things:

> **1. an apostrophe (') + s in the singular**
> EXAMPLE: *One **student's** phone was lost.*
>
> **2. an s + an apostrophe (') in the plural**
> EXAMPLE: *Two **students'** friendship lasted 50 years.*

Typical Screw-Ups

Beginning writers often confuse possessives with plurals, because they both end with the letter *s*.

> WRONG: *Martin Lawrence starred in the movie* Big **Mommas** House.
>
> RIGHT: <u>Martin Lawrence starred in the movie *Big Momma's House*</u>.

> WRONG: *Jack Nicholson starred in the movie* One Flew Over the **Cuckoos** Nest.
>
> RIGHT: <u>Jack Nicholson starred in the movie *One Flew Over the Cuckoo's Nest.*</u>

*In these examples, the words *momma's* and *cuckoo's* are in the possessive case. If you didn't have the apostrophe, you would think that there were more than one momma and more than one cuckoo, and you might think that the words *house* and *nest* were verbs rather than nouns. Confusing, right?

So that's why we need the apostrophes. By showing possession, they help keep things clear. They show who owns what.

Some Weird Exceptions

Not every noun adds an s to become plural, and that's the reason for a couple of exceptions:

SINGULAR: *The **man's** fingers were frostbitten.*
PLURAL: *The **men's** boss disappeared.*

SINGULAR: *The **woman's** sister called her.*
PLURAL: *The **women's** movement began in the 19th century.*
PLURAL: ***People's** attitudes about cussing have changed over the last 50 years.*

A Few More Rules

1. Nouns ending in *s* or *z* just need an apostrophe.
Nouns already ending in s or z can simply take an apostrophe, or if they're singular you can opt to add an apostrophe (') plus another "s." It's your choice.
EXAMPLES: *That's Ms. **Jones'** umbrella. That's Ms. **Jones's** umbrella.*

2. Personal pronouns NEVER take an apostrophe in the possessive case.
EXAMPLE: *An email of **his** said that a classmate of **yours** will never talk to a friend of **ours**.*

EXAMPLE: *It's about time that the company admitted **its** mistake.*

Possessive nouns can be singular or plural, and how you punctuate it tells us the difference. *The player's representative* speaks for one person. *The players' representative* speaks for a whole league. Which do you mean?

Reminders

By itself the letter s isn't enough to show possession. You must have an apostrophe, too—normally before the s if it's singular, after the s if it's plural. Without that crucial piece of punctuation, we can't tell what your nouns are up to, and we can't understand what you're trying to say.

Related References

See nouns in "The 8 Parts of Speech" (p. 9).

Test Yourself

Correct any ungrammatical sentences:

1. Alicia Keys song "A Womans Worth" was released in 2002.

2. The womans husband shaved his head during his wifes chemo treatments for cancer.

3. The Rolling Stones 1966 song "Mothers Little Helper" was about drug abuse.

4. *American Idols* first season began in the summer of 2002.

5. Quincy Jones daughter Rashida Jones once starred in NBCs hit sitcom *The Office*.

6. The cops patrol car hit the womans Jeep.

7. Stocks soared on Wall Street yesterday, when both companies first-quarter earnings were announced.

8. It's about time the team and it's coach tried something new.

9. We showed them our CDs, then traded them ours for theirs'.

10. The Williams' sisters rivalry goes beyond the tennis court.

❾
CASE PROBLEMS

I, Me, or Whom?

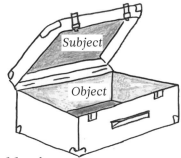

Why the problem?

You won't know whether to write *I* or *me* if you don't know the difference between a subject and an object.

What's the difference?

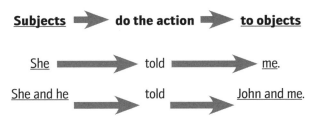

Subjects ➡ **do the action** ➡ **to objects**

She ➡ told ➡ me.

She and he ➡ told ➡ John and me.

In the first example, *she* is the subject, *told* is the verb, and *me* is the object. You wouldn't say *she told I. I* is the subject (nominative) form of the pronoun. It's never an object, regardless of how many other subjects there are. By contrast, *me* is always the object form, regardless of how many other objects there are.

9. CASE PROBLEMS

A common mistake

WRONG: *She told John and I.*

RIGHT: <u>She told John and</u> **me**.

People make this mistake because they remember hearing somewhere to say *John and I* (rather than *me and John*). That's right when John and I are the subjects. It's wrong when they're the objects. Actually, they've misremembered the lesson. It wasn't really about *I* vs. *me*. It was actually about *John* vs. *me*, about putting the other person first and yourself second, which is a matter of etiquette, not grammar. *I* vs. *me*? That's grammar, and there's only one right way.

Review of cases

Subject	I	you	he	she	it	we	they	who
Possessive	my	your	his	her	its	our	their	whose
Object	me	you	him	her	it	us	them	whom

Consider yourself lucky. In some languages there are five or six different cases. English has only three, and there's repetition in some of these (with *you*, *her*, and *it*) so less to memorize.

Follow this chart with mathematical precision when you're writing, and you'll be fine.

Note that none of these pronouns has an apostrophe in the possessive. *It's* means it is—always. *Its* is the possessive. And *its'* does not exist!

Some more examples

Glance at the chart as you read over these examples:

1. Tell (*I, me*) the truth. (*I, Me*) am telling you the truth.

2. You'll never guess what (*he, him*) said to Jack and (*she,* her).

3. (*Who's, Whose*) coming with (*we, us*)?

4. (*Who, Whom*) did she thank when she won the award?

5. (*They, Them*) and (*she, her*) bought coffee for (*he, him*) and (*I, me*).

Two tips

If you're not sure something's an object, find the verb and ask yourself who's doing it. In example #5, the verb is *bought*. Who did the buying? *They* and *she* did, so they're subjects.

Nouns or pronouns are objects in two circumstances: (1) when they're receiving the action or (2) when they're the objects of prepositions. So the preposition *for* is a **big signal** in example #5 that what follows will be an object. *She bought coffee for him; she bought it for me. She came with us.* Objects can't be subjects, right? So if you see a preposition, what follows will always be an object.

More help with *who* v. *whom*

Who is the subject form and *whom* is the object form.

SUBJECT FORM: *Who will come to the party?*

OBJECT FORM: *Whom did you invite?*

In the first example, *who* is the subject. We know that because it's the subject that's doing the action (*will come*). In the second example, *whom* is the object; it's not doing the inviting.

You are doing the inviting, so the pronoun *you* is obviously the subject.

Another way to figure out the case is to answer the question. If the answer to the first example is *she will come*, then *she* is the subject, just as *who* is. The answer to the second example might be this: *I invited him* or *I invited <u>her</u>*. So you need an object, and *whom* is what you need.

If you're still unsure

Language always changes, and the good news is that in 50 years whom will probably disappear. So let me give you a very practical piece of advice:

> If you don't know whether to use *who* or *whom*, go with the first (*who*), because it's becoming increasingly accepted and because nothing looks dumber than to use *whom* incorrectly.

Using *whom* incorrectly is like saying, "**Give it to John and I.**" It's an extra effort in the wrong direction, and it stands out and shouts for attention. It still pays to know the difference, and every good writer should, but don't wield *whom* if you don't know what you're doing. It'll kick you from behind.

Test yourself

Circle the correct word.

1. Please give (she, her) and (I, me) the tickets.

2. That's between you and (I, me).

3. I'm doing this for (he, him) and (she, her).

4. (They, them) and (she, her) will be going with you and (he, him).

5. Thanks for standing by (he, him) and (I, me).

6. (Who's, Whose) bike is this?

7. (Who, Whom) did you go with?

8. (Who's, Whose) to blame for this?

9. (Who, Whom) are you fooling?

10. (Who, Whom) are they taking to the beach?

CAPITALIZATION ⑩ Aa

Why bother?

Languages like German capitalize every noun. English doesn't do that anymore. Instead, we just capitalize "proper" nouns, especially names—names of people, cities, companies, books, movies, and so on. Capital letters allow words to stand out from the pack. That lets your meaning get across quickly. But there are a few other times when you capitalize.

The rules

Four circumstances trigger capital letters:

1. proper nouns (names)

2. titles

3. the first word of a sentence

4. the first word of a full quotation

Names (Category 1)

Erika, FedEx, Coca-Cola, September, Tuesday, Christmas, Chicago

NOTE 1: If a company doesn't capitalize its name (for example, *ebay*), then you shouldn't either.

NOTE 2: Some words may be capitalized if they're used as part of a person's title. [See below.]

Proper or generic names?

GENERIC: *He wants to be the town's mayor.*

PROPER: *On Tuesday <u>Mayor</u> Mark Luttrell held a press conference.*

GENERIC: *I went to see a doctor.*

PROPER: *She heard that <u>Dr</u>. Patrick Smith treats patients for free.*

GENERIC: *He was the first governor to support the bill.*

PROPER: *According to the newspaper, <u>Gov</u>. Phil Bredesen supports the bill.*

Titles (Category 2)

Capitalizing words in titles draws the eye and highlights the work. It isn't mandatory, but it's quite common and very helpful because it sets the title off clearly from the rest of the text. That's a courtesy readers appreciate. So you'll see this format for the names and subsections of many published documents, the titles of broadcast programs and a lot of other mass media fare:

books (*Angela's Ashes, The DaVinci Code*)

academic papers ("Radio Pioneers in the Southeast")

journal articles ("Two Views of Versailles: A New Approach")

short stories ("Down at the River")

poems ("I Wandered Lonely as a Cloud")

songs ("Round Midnight")

news stories ("Mayor Will Fight New Proposal")

movies (*True Grit, The King's Speech*)

TV programs (Fox's *The Simpsons*, CBS' *60 Minutes*)

Web pieces ("The Roots of the Financial Meltdown")

NOTE 1: You generally capitalize only substantive words and not small prepositions (*in, to*) and articles (*a, the*), unless they lead the title.

NOTE 2: Names of books, newspapers, magazines, movies, and TV shows are italicized. Names of the chapters in books, the articles in newspapers and magazines, the episodes of TV programs, and songs are put in quotation marks.

The first word of a sentence (Category 3)

Just as a period signals the end of one sentence, a capitalized word indicates the start of another.

The movie just ended. We're thinking about seeing a second film. Do you want to join us?

A semicolon doesn't end a sentence; it's used within one. So you don't capitalize the first word after a semicolon because you're not beginning a new sentence, just a new clause.

The first word of a full quotation (Category 4)

Partial quotations incorporate a quoted word into the writer's sentence, so it's not normally capitalized. Full quotations are a different matter, however. They usually begin with a capital letter.

PARTIAL OR PARAPHRASE

He said he wouldn't.

He said that wasn't his "take on the matter."

FULL, FORMAL

He said, "No."

She said, "That's crazy."

The soldier replied, "If that's what it takes, that's what we'll do."

Related References

See next chapter, "Errors Punctuating Quotations."

Test yourself

Mark the examples that contain errors, and fix them.

1. we haven't seen the movie yet; It just came out.

2. The Mayor said, "it's not an easy issue but one that will take a long time to figure out."

3. She saw the movie *scream*. have you seen it?

4. I heard him say dr. Gordon will be here in a few minutes.

5. Do you usually use fedex or ups?

6. Have you read the book *to kill a mockingbird*?

7. The mayor said he'd like to run for governor.

8. Have you ever been to new york in october?

9. *The sound and the fury* is a novel by william faulkner.

10. He told her he was "sorry," then wrote, "you can't believe how much I miss you."

11
ERRORS PUNCTUATING QUOTATION

"Please don't quote me," he said.

Punctuation rules

RULE #1 — Full, formal quotations require punctuation.

He said, "I'm going even if there's a traffic jam."
$\uparrow$

RULE #2 — Partial quotes and paraphrases generally don't.

He said he was going "even if there's a traffic jam."

He said he couldn't "believe this gorgeous weather."

He said that he was "100% opposed."

RULE #3 — Commas and periods go inside, not outside, quotation marks. [See p. 71.]

He said, "I can't believe this gorgeous weather."
$\uparrow$

RULE #4 — Multi-sentence quotations require a colon.

He said: "I'm going even if there's a traffic jam. I don't care what the streets are like."

Note that the attribution should go before, not after, these long quotations.

RULE #5 — Use brackets to insert a word not originally in the quotation.

He said, "I can't believe [the mayor] did that."

(American) Rules for Punctuating Quotations

INSIDE	OUTSIDE	DEPENDS
" " ,	" " ;	" ! " .
" " .	" " :	" " !
		" ? " .
		" " ?
commas, periods	semicolons, colons	exclamation points, question marks

A few tricks

You can vary *how* you use quotations by putting the **attribution** part (*he says*, *she says*) at the beginning, in the middle, or at the end of the sentence.

- AT THE START: **He said**, "I'm going even if there's a traffic jam."

- IN THE MIDDLE: "I'm going," **he said**, "even if there's a traffic jam."

- AT THE END: "I'm going even if there's a traffic jam," **he said**.

Avoid a comma splice

Using a comma before a direct, one-sentence quotation is the accepted convention for handling quotes. It may look like a comma splice, but it's not.

Many inexperienced writers, however, wind up with a comma splice when they put the attribution between *two main clauses* (two sentences).

> COMMA SPLICE: *"I'm going even if there's a traffic jam," he said, "I don't care what the streets are like."*

> CORRECTED: *"I'm going even if there's a traffic jam," he said. "I don't care what the streets are like."*

In this example, the attribution can go with the first sentence or the second sentence but not both—unless it's put at the beginning with a colon.

Two reminders

1. You'll generally never see the word *that* before a full, formal quotation. (If you do, it's probably a mistake.) As a result, it usually doesn't come with punctuation:

    WRONG: *She said, that was "only fair."*

    WRONG: *She said that, was "only fair."*

    RIGHT: *She said that was "only fair."*

    That is mostly used in *partial* quotations and paraphrases.

2. So with full, formal quotation, there are two obvious signals: **punctuation** <u>and</u> a **capital letter** at the beginning of the quote. Punctuation and a capital letter go together as a team.

Test yourself

Correct the following sentences.

1. Tanya says; "Where will they put them? The city has no idea."

2. Daniel added, "It's our job to go out and get the job ourselves. It doesn't mean anything if it's given to us."

3. Williams, a graphic design major, said that in his field, "that would be great to get that kind of experience."

4. She said, "I can't believe you did that".

5. "What do you call that", he asked.

6. "It's a great opportunity," she said, "I can't wait to start."

7. He told the cashier he, "loved the CD."

8. "This food is cold" he told the waiter.

9. The soldier looked at the captain and said, he was ready.

10. "I've been in Atlanta for a week," she said "I'm ready to go home."

HYPHEN HELL

What do hyphens do?

Hyphens link words and put them together to form more complex packages. They also let the reader know what you're doing, so it makes comprehension easier.

When do you need them?

You need a hyphen when you lump nouns or adjectives together as one item that'll describe another.

> NO HYPHEN NEEDED: *The board is nine feet long.*
> HYPHEN NEEDED: *That's a nine-foot board.*
>
> NO HYPHEN NEEDED: *She is 25 years old.*
> HYPHEN NEEDED: *She's a 25-year-old woman.*
>
> NO HYPHEN NEEDED: *He's often in your face.*
> HYPHEN NEEDED: *He uses an in-your-face approach.*
>
> NO HYPHEN NEEDED: *Four cars collided.*
> HYPHEN NEEDED: *It was a four-car collision.*

NO HYPHEN NEEDED: *She can do whatever's asked.*
HYPHEN NEEDED: *She has a can-do attitude.*

NO HYPHEN NEEDED: *Police raided the house late at night.*
HYPHEN NEEDED: *Police conducted a late-night raid on the house.*

So when the words are bunched together to modify another word or phrase, you need a hyphen. When they don't serve that function, you don't.

When do you NOT need a hyphen?

When one of the words you're combining in the package is an –*ly* **adverb**, you don't usually need one.

NO HYPHEN NEEDED: *They both made strongly compelling arguments.*

NO HYPHEN NEEDED: *That's a quickly developing problem.*
HYPHEN NEEDED: *That's a fast-developing problem.*

When the words are part of a **name**, the hyphen is omitted.

NO HYPHEN NEEDED: That's a Black & Decker tool.

When the words are part of a **frequently used phrase**, you can often leave out the hyphen.

NO HYPHEN NEEDED: The city council vote took place last night.

Here the term "city council" is used so often that it has almost become a name unto itself. Sometimes these examples are judgment calls. When in doubt, insert the hyphen.

Reminders

Hyphens join two or more words to form single units. They also help guide and orient your reader. Without them, we can't figure out why you have so many nouns or adjectives crowded together in your sentence.

Test yourself

In the following sentences some phrases are grammatically correct, while others lack hyphens when they need them. Identify and fix the latter.

1. He's the know it all type.

2. After driving three or four miles, I saw an old fashioned chain gang cutting grass.

3. She was telling us about a bar with a two drink minimum.

4. Was there an increase in the number of minimum wage jobs in Memphis last year?

5. The Glock 37 is a .45 caliber pistol.

6. Philo T. Farnsworth, the inventor of electronic television, was just 14 years old when he sketched his first camera design.

7. The point guard made his fourth three point shot in a row.

8. She described her neighbor this way: "He's a comic book freak, a Black Sabbath fanatic, a tattoo covered teenager, and maybe the coolest kid I know."

9. The buzzer sounded the two minute warning.

10. My computer has high speed access.

OTHER MATTERS

CONFUSED WORDS & COMMON MISSPELLINGS

English is a big, rich language, and there are a lot of words that sound alike but mean very different things. Whole books are dedicated to these tricky monsters. This chapter highlights only a few—the ones that are the most common source of angst, confusion, and fear.

Its and It's

No possessive adjective or pronoun (*my, mine, your, yours, our, ours, his, her, hers, its, theirs, whose*) takes an apostrophe. When you see *it's*, that's a contraction and it always means *it is*. Always! (And **its'** doesn't exist!)

IT'S = IT IS

CONTRACTION: It's about time you got here.
POSSESSIVE: Its color is blue.

Affect and Effect

There are two obscure exceptions, but 99% of the time *affect* is a verb and *effect* is a noun.

VERB: Her words affected the audience.

NOUN: Her words had an effect on the audience.

How do you remember the difference? Get creative. But you might think of *affect* as if it were *infect* and treat *effect* as if it were *defect.*

Sit and Set

Sit, meaning to take a seat, is a verb that does not take an object. *I need to sit. Please sit down. She's sitting right now.*

Set, meaning to put or place, is a verb that **does** take an object. *Set it down. Please set the table.*

Lie and Lay

There are actually three verbs here, and it's best just to memorize them and the way they're conjugated.

Meaning	(*not to tell the truth*)	(*to be on your back, to recline*)	(*to set or put something down*)
Present tense	lie	lie	lay
Simple past tense	lied	lay	laid
Past perfect tense	has or have **lied**	has or have **lain**	has or have **laid**

The first and the third verbs are the easiest to remember because their forms are the same in two of the tenses. Note also that *lay* is a transitive verb, meaning it takes an object.

Examples: *The chicken laid an egg. Please lay the phone on the table.*

There, Their, and They're

There is usually an adverb or a pronoun.

> *He drove there.*
> *There is a fly in my soup.*

> Think of the phrase "Hey, there."

Their is a possessive adjective.

> *The students took their exams this week.*
> *The players won their first game yesterday.*

They're is a contraction of they are. (Remember that possessive adjectives never take apostrophes, so this is not one.)

> *They're not coming to the restaurant.*
> *They're probably the best two players in the league.*

Test yourself

Circle the correct choice in each sentence.

1. After working all day, she (lied, lay, laid, lain) down in front of the TV.

2. He (lied, lay, laid, lain) the book on the table.

3. I have never (lied, lay, laid, lain) by the pool for more than two hours.

4. If (there, their, they're) is one thing I can't stand, (its, it's) dishonesty.

5. (There, Their, They're) car is being repaired right now. (Its, It's) alternator isn't working.

6. I heard that (there, their, they're) planning a party for Carrie.

7. Won't you (sit, set) down?

8. You can (sit, set) the bag by my locker.

9. The talk show host's words had little (affect, effect) on his listeners.

10. Do you know how that medication will (affect, effect) you?

CONCLUSION

FIVE ESSENTIAL TIPS

The bottom line in writing well is caring enough about your reputation to get things right. If you want to express yourself clearly and simply, you can't afford mistakes, so follow the suggestions below for the best prose possible.

1. Use a dictionary!

Only bush-leaguers and mistake-prone amateurs write without one. Here's where you find out if you spelled something correctly and if you used the right word. Every good writer needs a dictionary within reach of the computer. And whether it's a printed volume or an online version, use a reliable one. *Billy Bob's Web Dictionary* isn't as trustworthy as the *American Heritage Dictionary*.

2. Read aloud.

You'd be surprised how many glitches you can clean up just by hearing your sentences, as opposed to seeing them. Frequently, your ear catches errors your eye misses. Part of that is because you're forced to slow down. Part of it is that our brains work differently with sounds than they do with sights.

3. Enlarge the text while you're editing.

This also makes it more likely we'll notice mistakes. As with reading aloud, we're trying to compensate for the fact that most of us are very fast, superficial readers.

4. Put the copy aside for an hour or a day and come back to it later.

When you're in the middle of doing something, you often lose perspective on it. Sometimes you get tired or sloppy. Either way, your eyes and ears stop working as they should. So try to take a break from your work, because that allows you to return with your senses refreshed. It also restores your judgment and allows you to read something as if for the first time, as if someone else wrote it. This is when you feel most like a member of the intended audience, which heightens your editorial instincts.

5. Edit again and again.

Okay, sometimes a story or paper or memo is just due when it's due. So you might not have the luxury of infinite rounds of editing. That's probably a good thing. Otherwise, nobody would ever finish anything. But you're not really going to damage the quality of a piece of writing—and certainly not the grammar— by repeated editing. If anything, you'll simply catch things you missed the last time. So take advantage of extra time to go over your writing. When you catch that spelling mistake or misplaced comma, you'll be glad you did.

- What's the most effective, powerful, and permanent solution? **Read a lot**.

THE FINAL WORD

Everybody—writers, editors and teachers included—makes mistakes. We're human, after all. Learning grammar won't mean you'll never make errors again. The point is simply to reduce their likelihood and decrease their frequency. So relax a little. You won't be perfect in this life. But you can be better, a lot better. Of course, improving isn't what average people do. But why be average? Average is boring.

RECOMMENDED READING

Here are nine terrific books on grammar. Most are comprehensive. The three that are not, *The Elements of Style, Woe Is I,* and *Eats, Shoots, and Leaves* are shorter, more personal contributions. As such, they won't answer every question but are eclectic and fun to read. Every writer should have at least one comprehensive grammar reference.

Associated Press Stylebook. Cambridge, Mass.: Perseus, 2007.

Chicago Manual of Style. 15th edition. Chicago: University of Chicago Press, 2003.

Hodges, John C. et al. *Harbrace College Handbook.* 13th edition. New York: Harcourt Brace Jovanovich, 1998.

Kessler, Lauren and Duncan McDonald, *When Words Collide: A Media Writer's Guide to Grammar and Style.* Boston: Thomson Wadsworth, 2004.

O'Conner, Patricia T. *Woe Is I: The Grammarphobe's Guide to Better English in Plain English.* New York: Riverhead Books, 1996.

Strunk, William, Jr., and E.B. White. *The Elements of Style.* 4th edition. Boston: Allyn & Bacon, 1999.

Truss, Lynne, *Eats, Shoots & Leaves.* New York: Gotham Books, 2003.

Turabian, Kate L. A *Manual for Writers of Term Papers, Theses, and Dissertations.* 6th edition. Chicago: University of Chicago Press, 1996.

Watkins, Floyd C. and William B. Dillingham, *Practical English Handbook.* 9th edition. Boston: Houghton Mifflin, 1991.

Ch. 1—Sentence Fragments

1. Sentence
2. Fragment
3. Fragment
4. Fragment
5. Sentence
6. Sentence
7. Sentence
8. Fragment
9. Fragment
10. Sentence

Ch. 2—Fused Sentences

1. The police arrested a suspect last night, but they haven't yet released his name.
2. Here is the money I owe. You can use it for whatever you want.
3. "I feel good; I knew that I would." —James Brown
4. He asked her out, and I heard she said, "No, but dream on."
5. My roommate bought all this beer; therefore it's now my favorite.
6. Give me a break. I don't know.
7. Houston's point guard scored 28 points; the power forward turned in a dozen more.
8. The Marine sniper set the scope on his M40, and then he squeezed the trigger.
9. I emailed you last week although now you're getting back to me.
10. She's going to law school, and her sister is a licensed electrician.

Ch. 3—Comma Splices

1. Comma splice
2. Comma splice
3. Correct
4. Comma splice
5. Comma splice
6. Comma splice
7. Correct
8. Comma splice
9. Correct
10. Comma splice

Ch. 4—Other Comma Problems

1. The company was founded on March 12, 1974, in Milwaukee Wisconsin.
2. Well, that's what you think.
3. Dad, can you hear me now?
4. (Correct) Go, team!
5. Her husband, Mike, joined us at the restaurant.
6. Barack Obama, the 44th president of the United States, was born in Hawaii.
7. Derrick wants to be a stand-up comic, which is not what you'd expect from him.
8. Governor John Smith visited our city during the summer.
9. (Correct) Jay-Z, whose real name is Shawn Carter, grew up in Brooklyn.
10. The movie made $60 million over the weekend, which wasn't a surprise to those of us who saw it.

Ch. 5—Misplaced Modifiers

1. Heading upstairs to escape the smell of detergents, visitors are drawn to the north side of the floor, where they go down a hall with shields hanging at eye-level.

2. Looking around, you see that almost every table is filled with at least one person.

3. Students rest on benches, read books, and sit on sidewalks as they browse their laptops.

4. In the center of the room sits an elderly woman, eating chicken and constantly turning her head from left to right as she watches others.

5. They are all dressed in team uniforms and talking among themselves.

6. While standing outside, the man watched in horror for 15 minutes.

7. Students walked silently into the library.

8. She donated old clothes and several cans of food, along with a new bicycle, to the shelter.

9. We had a great time singing and dancing, not to mention catching up with old friends, at the party.

10. My dad videotaped the tornado's destructive path as the storm tore through the city and ripped the roof off a restaurant.

Ch. 6—Subject-Verb Mismatches

1. "Joints & Jam" is the name of a song by the Black Eyed Peas.

2. My friends all like the movie. My girlfriend does, too.

3. Economics is the first subject I got a C in at school.

4. The reasons for her reaction are simple: I let her down.

5. Either he or John goes, or you and she go.

6. The days of summer are almost over.

7. Thirty pounds of high-grade marijuana were confiscated in the raid.

8. The best argument for these ideas was missed by bloggers and mainstream journalists alike.

9. You're joking, right?

10. Two players on the team were suspended last night.

Ch. 7—Subject-Pronoun Mismatches

1. Ask most people, and they'll tell you they love junk food.

2. No workers want to lose their job.

3. The sorority tried to raise money for its favorite charity.

4. A spokesperson for the group said it would try to reschedule.

5. Everyone deserves a fair opportunity.

6. The Senate passed the bill unanimously, the first time its members agreed on anything all year.

7. The board shared its views before the vote.

8. Is someone in a bad mood?